D0309592

30p

H 30/10 wlbn

Pam Ayres

Thoughts of a
Late-Night Knitter

Illustrated by Roy Garnham Elmore

Arrow Books

Thoughts of a Late-Night Knitter

Also in Arrow by Pam Ayres

SOME OF ME POETRY
SOME MORE OF ME POETRY

ARROW BOOKS

Arrow Books Ltd
3 Fitzroy Square, London W1P 6JD

An imprint of the Hutchinson Publishing Group

London Melbourne Sydney Auckland Wellington
Johannesburg and agencies throughout the world

First published by Arrow Books Ltd 1978
© Pam Ayres 1978
Illustrations © Roy Garnham Elmore

Typeset in English Times by J and K Hybert, Maidenhead
Printed and bound in England by
Petty & Sons Ltd, Leeds

ISBN 0 09 918660 8

for my family with love

Contents

Clamp the Mighty Limpet

I am Clamp the Mighty Limpet
I am solid, I am stuck
I am welded to the rockface
With my superhuman suck
I live along the waterline
And in the dreary caves
I am Clamp the Mighty Limpet
I am Ruler of the Waves.

What care I for the shingle,
For the dragging of the tide,
With my unrelenting sucker
And my granite underside?
There's only one reward
For those who come to prise at me
And that's to watch their fingernails
As they go floating out to sea.

Don't upset *me*, I'm a limpet
Though it's plankton I devour
Be very, very careful
I can move an inch an hour!
Don't you poke or prod me
For I warn you — if you do
You stand there for a fortnight
And I might be stuck on you!

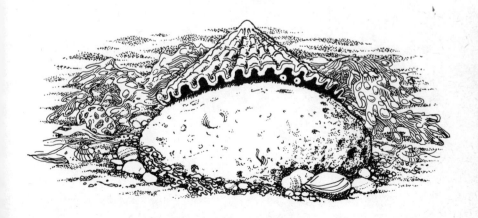

I Don't Want to go to School Mum

I don't want to go to school Mum
I want to stay at home with my duck.
I'd rather stay at home with you Mum,
And hit the skirting board with my truck.
Don't make me go to school today Mum,
I'll sit here quiet on the stairs
Or I'll sit underneath the table
Scratching all the varnish off the chairs.

I don't want to go to school Mum
When I could be underneath your feet.
It's shopping day and we could go together
Taking twice as long to get to Regent Street.
And every time you stop to talk to someone
I won't let you concentrate, no fear,
I'll be jumping up and down beside you
Shouting, "Can I have some sweets Mum?" in your ear.

Or how about me doing a bit of painting?
Or what about a bit of cutting out?
Or sitting in the open bedroom window,
Body in and legs sticking out?
Or what about us going up the park Mum?
Or how about me sitting at the sink?
Or what about me making you a cake Mum?
And Mum. Hey Mum. Mum can I have a drink?

And Mum, Mum what's that at the bottom of the cupboard?
And Mum, what's in the bag you put down there?
And hey Mum watch me jump straight off the sofa,
And Mum, whose dog is that stood over there?
What you doing Mum? Peeling potatoes?
Sit me on the drainer watching you
I wouldn't *mind* me trousers getting wet Mum.
Oh I aren't half fed up. What can I do?

What time is Daddy coming home Mum?
What's in that long packet? Sausagemeat?
How long is it before he comes Mum?
And Mum. Hey Mum. What can I have to eat?
Oh sorry Mum! I've upset me Ribena.
Oh look! It's making quite a little pool.
Hey Mum, hey, where we going in such a hurry?
Oh Mum! Hey Mum, you're taking me to SCHOOL!

Puppy Problems

I bought myself a puppy
And I hoped in time he might
Become my friend and ward off
Things that go bump in the night,
So I put him in a shoe box
And at home I took him out,
And then began to learn
What owning puppies is about.

I tried so hard to love him
And I didn't rave and shout
As he bit into the sofa
And he dragged the stuffing out.
I *gave* him things to chew
But soon I couldn't fail to see
That he liked the things he *found*
More than the things supplied by me.

He frayed my lovely carpet
That I'd saved my pennies for,
And when he wasn't chewing
He was weeing on the floor.
Nor did he spare the table leg
That came in for a gnaw,
Though I told him off the message
Never seemed to reach his jaw.

We laboured at the gardening,
Me and my little pup.
At two I planted flowers
And at four he dug them up.
He liked to dig, he'd bury bones
And pat it down so neat,
And then he'd rush indoors
As clods of mud flew off his feet.

I bought a book on training
And I read it all one night,
And when we set off out
I really thought we'd got it right,
With titbits in my coat
To give him once he got the knack,
But he didn't so I couldn't
So *I* ate them coming back.

When I commanded "Heel!"
He never seemed to take the point
But galloped on half-strangled,
Tugging my arm out of joint.
He jumped up people's clothes,
The cleaning bills I had to pay!
And when I shouted "Here!"
He turned and ran the other way.

One day I drove him over
And I gave him to my Dad
Who welcomed him and trained him,
But it left me very sad.
So I thought I'd let you know
In case a pup's in store for you
That it's very wise indeed
To have a Dad who likes dogs too.

9

Clive the Fearless Birdman

Clive the fearless birdman was convinced that he could fly.
At night he lay in bed and dreamed of soaring through the sky,
Of cruising through the clouds, of winging far out into space
And he had a leather helmet with a beak stuck on the face.

Clive the fearless birdman had a wife who did not care
For his fly-by-night ambition of cavorting through the air.
With mocking and with ridicule she did her best to kill it,
And cruelly filled his breakfast plate with cuttlefish and millet.

But in his little potting shed he'd built some mighty wings
Out of balsa wood and sticky tape and plasticine and strings.
Up to his neck in feathers which had taken months to pluck
He laboured with his Evo-Stick, he fashioned and he stuck.

He tried it on at last and slowly turned from side to side,
So wonderful was it that Clive the birdman slumped and cried.
So shiny were the feathers all in silver grey and black,
With eiderdown all up the front and turkey down the back.

It strapped on with a harness buckled round his arms and throat,
All made adjustable to fit the thickness of his coat.
Just to see him walking in the street made women shriek
As he flapped by in his harness and his helmet and his beak.

So Clive announced to all the culmination of his search
And told the local papers he'd be jumping off the church.
Seth, the old gravedigger, with his face as black as coal
Said, "If he jumps off the steeple I shan't have to dig a hole."

And so the day arrived and all the people came to stare,
Police held back the crowds and all the local press was there.
Clive read out a noble speech, an address to the people
That nobody could hear for it was windy up the steeple.

He stepped out in the sky and flapped his wings just for a minute,
Far above the vicar's garden as he plummeted straight in it.
He lay there in the cabbages without another flutter
And the beak came off his helmet and went rolling in the gutter.

But far away in Heaven Clive the birdman reigns supreme,
Soaring through the air without the aid of jet or steam,
So at the Pearly Gates if it's with Clive you wish to speak,
You can tell him by his harness and his helmet and his beak.

Will Anybody Marry Me?

Will anybody marry me?
I would not cost him dear,
I am in perfect nick
And good condition for the year.
He would not have to be a Mr World
Built like Fort Knox
For I would do the plastering
And saw up all the blocks.

Will anybody marry me?
I would be awful sweet,
I'd let him knock me glasses off
And kick them down the street,
And I would not be a nagger
Saying, "Will you paint the pelmet?"
And if he was a fireman
I would never dent his helmet.

And concerning older girls
Our inhibitions have all gone,
And me dad's an electrician
So I'd really turn him on,
Now I cannot give my telephone
That's hazardous I know
But if anyone will have me
It is Bognor 410.

13

Bournemouth

He was long and tall and thin and dull
And so was she,
He dried his trim moustache
When they had drunk their China tea.
And he was very quiet, very rich
And rather kind,
With one eye that could see
And with the other, which was blind.

His hair was rather sandy
And his manner rather terse,
His clothes were very dull and safe
But then, well, so were hers.
Her shoes were very dear
And never purchased on a whim,
They toned in with the wardrobe
And it was the same with him.

She couldn't really claim,
That as he read the *Business News*
And regaled her now and then
With his opinions and views,
That his figure was endearing
In the fat expensive chair,
Flecked about with dandruff
From his thin and sandy hair.

And neither in his heart
Could he blossom and rejoice
To listen to her speaking
In her flat and toneless voice,
To watch her rosebud mouth
Which would habitually melt
Into a little smile
She always smiled but never felt.

But they got along together
And they liked the same shampoo,
And he was so polite
With "Oh dear lady: After you!"
And when they walked on Sunday
He would always take her hand
And hold it like a cold dead fish
Washed up along the strand.

Most weekends you could see him
Striding out across the links,
While she would be presiding
By the double drainer sinks,
Concocting gourmet meals
But ritualistic, free of mirth,
Rosé and white and lobster bright
And things that cost the earth.

And as she whipped the cream
And folded in a little more
She saw the dark-eyed sailors
As they lingered on the shore,
And he sat on the verandah
With his *Telegraph* and *Punch*
And watched the young girls laughing
As he waited for his lunch.

Ever Since I Had me Op

Hello, it's nice to see you looking well,
What? How am I?
I haven't been so good myself
But I've been getting by.
Yes, I've had a bit of trouble
Well, I wouldn't bore a friend
But if you knew how much I'd suffered
Well, your hair would stand on end.

No, I'm not one to complain
And we all have our cross to bear,
And I wouldn't even tell you
What they did to me in there.
If you asked how many stitches
I wouldn't let it cross my lips,
Well all right then, twenty-seven
And that's not including clips.

Course, it was only fifty-fifty,
On the drip all night and day.
Oh they gave me all the lot
And then they took it all away.
You wouldn't have recognized me
And I'm glad I never seen ya
And the doctor on the case
Gave up and went back home. To Kenya.

Well, I know you're in a hurry
And you haven't time to stop,
And I've just seen Deirdre,
She'll want to know about me op.
And there's always someone worse off
Than yourself, without a doubt,
In my case I haven't met him
But I'm sure that he's about.

And you're healthy dear, enjoy it
For it fades away so soon,
Now I've got me eighteen pills
So I'll get through this afternoon.
Don't give a thought to how I've suffered
I'm the last one to complain,
And I'll keep on smiling through it all
Until we meet again.

17

The Dreadful Accident
with the Kitchen Scissors

I gave my lovely Teddy bear a haircut,
For Mother, she had sent me for a trim
And really, I felt that much better for it
I thought that I would do the same for him.
I picked him up and grabbed the kitchen scissors,
"Just a snip or two, old bear," I said,
But I find I was not cut out as a barber,
For accidentally, I tore his head.

I do not criticize the man who stuffed him,
He had to do it thoroughly no doubt,
But I wish he had not stuffed the head so solid
Then I could stop the stuffing coming out.
I've been to wrap me bear's head in a turban,
Well, he's been dressed up like it for a week.
Mum asked me, "What's he got that round his head for?"
I said: "He's a bus conductor... He's a Sikh!"

But how long can I keep up the deception?
Where his face was plump it's sunken in
And though he's very hard across the forehead
He's turning very soft around the chin!
I haven't dared to look beneath his turban,
I know it's just a mass of coloured foam,
And Mother's started looking very puzzled
As she picks up bits of it around the home.

And Auntie Greta's coming here for dinner,
And she's the one who gave the bear to me
And that is when my crime will be uncovered,
For I know that he won't stand much scrutiny.
Oh Mother, Auntie Greta, I'm so sorry!
I *tried* to sew his head up, I tried hard!
But as I said, they stuffed his head so tightly
That every stitch has stretched out half a yard!

I'm waiting by the door for Auntie Greta,
I rammed poor Teddy underneath the quilt,
And every time a car stops by our gateway
Both me knees start knocking from the guilt.
She's bound to say, "Now where's that lovely Teddy?"
And his head's all caving in... What shall I *do?*
Oh Crikey, here it is, a blue Marina...
Oh. Hello Auntie Greta... how are you?

Thoughts of a Late-Night Knitter

I had a lovely boyfriend,
Knit one, purl one.
Had him for a long time,
Cast on for the back.
Had him all the summer,
Loved him, cuddled him,
Push it up the knitting pin
And gather up the slack.

Well he *knew* how much I liked him,
Knit one, purl one.
I made him seven jerseys,
Never did him any wrong,
And he told me that he loved me,
Knit one, purl one.
Told me that he loved me
But he didn't stop for long.

Well, he never said he'd left me,
Knit one, purl one.
He never even told me
'Cause I found out on me own.
I was going up the chippie,
Knit one, purl one.
And he came out of the pictures
With that horrid Mary Stone.

Well I didn't know what hit me,
Knit one, slip one.
After I'd looked after him
It wasn't very nice,
And they went off down the High Street,
Laughin', gigglin',
And left me on the corner
With me chips as cold as ice.

Well, it isn't that I miss him
Knit one, drop one.
I never even think of him
Good riddance... ta ta!
I'm very independent!
Snap one, tie one.
I've never been so cheerful,
Ha ha... ha!

And I hear they're getting married,
Knit one, drop nine.
I wish them every happiness,
It's *lovely* staying in!
Well I don't need romancing,
Cuddlin', dancin'.
Bundle up the knitting bag
And sling it in the bin.

Rocking Gran Blues

Who says I'm too old for the disco?
While the music still touches me soul,
While I dance in bare feet and move with the beat
And me feet turn as black as the coal.
Oh just say the word young Adonis!
I'll reggae with you till it's day,
Just lend me a fag and pass us me bag
For me Pan Stick has all run away.

Oh yes, I know you've seen nothing like it!
My dancing is lissom and free!
Take a look round the place, each wondering face,
Everyone's looking at me!
Oh take it away, lay it on me!
We'll tear up the floor through the night,
We'll be rocking and reeling while the ball on the ceiling
Festoons us in speckles of light.

I've scraped all me hair in a beehive,
I've stapled it up at the back,
Though once it was pepper and salt, dear,
Now it is ebony black.
Tell the Deejay to turn up the volume!
Turn it up with no fear of reproof!
So we hear the pound and the pulsating sound
And the woodworm all fall out the roof.

For there's nothing like music to get you,
Oh the shivers it sends down your back,
And if you're approaching the bar, dear,
I'll have a nice rum and black.
And get me a packet of crisps, dear,
Bacon or onion will do
And then *mon amour* we'll give it what for
And dance till our faces turn blue.

And then in my clapped-out Ford Consul,
Parked by a rippling stream,
I'll flash you a smile, find the spot on the dial
And cover the windows with steam.
It's the wonderful weekend from working,
So until Monday when we clock on
Take my hand in the dark, out in the car park
It's Saturday evening: rock on.

After the Jubilee

Don't play anything else on your squeeze box Mother
To honour the Jubilee.
I daresay the Queen would enjoy it
But it has started grating on me.
Come and sit on this tattered old bunting,
Here's your tea in a Jubilee cup,
Don't play "God save the Queen" for a minute
Or in other words, Mother... shut up.

Ah but how we rose to the occasion
With our patriotism and flags,
With our parties and fêtes and processions
And our Jubilee carrier bags.
How we planned for the local street party
With the sun beating down on your head,
But unfortunately it rained on you and me
So we had it in Angus's shed.

But the dingy old street, how we decked it,
How the neighbours all chattered and talked
As they knocked the tin tacks in the Union Jacks
And the next day the whole lot had walked,
And the kiddies all rushed down to help us
Who's to say industry never pays?
They wrote, "Long may she reign" on the brickwork
And it did look, it poured down for days!

And the bonfires they lit in the village,
Well, we'll see nothing like it again,
And the only bonfire that burned brighter
Was the shock one up Arsonists Lane.
And we went on a torchlight procession
We all bought special torches for that.
I held mine up high, proudly up in the sky,
And me shoulders got covered in fat.

So before you strike up again Mother
Let me refill your Jubilee cup.
Me slab cake went down in the middle
But I've turned it the other way up.
The fireworks and fêtes are all over,
The street parties swept up and done.
Here's a message for Buckingham Palace,
Can we do it again? It was *fun!*

Little Nigel Gnasher

Little Nigel Gnasher was his name,
He bit his nails.
When other boys were having fights
Or finding slugs and snails,
You always knew that Nigel
Would be at his normal station,
Beside the rails he bit his nails
Eyes shut for concentration.

His mother tried to stop him
But young Nigel's ears were shut.
She wrapped his hands in woolly gloves,
But Nigel Gnasher cut
Straight through the woolly fabric
With his sharp and practised teeth
And bit the helpless fingernails
That sheltered underneath.

Mrs Gnasher took him
To the Doctor one fine day.
The Doctor looked at Nigel's nails
And quickly looked away,
Saying, "Calcium deficiency
Has laid these nails to waste."
And he gave the lad a bag of chalk
But he didn't like the taste.

Oh he bit them on the landing
And he bit them on the stair,
Nigel Gnasher bit his nails
Till there was nothing there,
Nigel Gnasher bit them
Till he couldn't stand the pain,
And then he'd summon up his courage
And bite them all again.

When other people rested
Hands outstretched on the settee,
Nigel sat upon his hands
So people wouldn't see.
He plastered them with Dettol,
Savlon, Germolene and more,
He'd have it done by half past one
And bite it off by four.

One day a local millionaire
Was driving round about.
He spotted Nigel Gnasher
And impulsively leaned out,
Crying, "Here's a present, sonny,
From eccentric Jeffrey Krupp,"
And a fiver hit the ground,
But Nigel *couldn't pick it up!*

And then the local bully,
Carver Clay, he came along
And though his head was short,
His fingernails were very long.
He pushed aside poor Nigel
Who lay clawing at the ground
And ran off with the fiver
Shouting, "Look what I have found!"

So the moral of this story,
Little Gnashers far and wide,
Is, don't bite them up the middle
And don't bite them down the side,
Don't bite them front or sideways,
Spare your poor nails from the habit,
Then if someone throws a fiver
They will be on hand to grab it!

A Tale of Two Settees

It was down at the furniture warehouse,
As I wandered one morning in May,
To buy a settee for the woodworm
Had eaten the old one away.
It was there in a flash that I saw him
In front of the chipboard veneer.
His Levis and shirt were covered in dirt
And he had a gold stud, in his ear.

I did not let on that I'd seen him
Oh no, for I played hard to get
Deliberating by the vinyl
And stroking the uncut moquette.
But he casually walked over to me
And seductively murmured, "Oi, oi,"
And there in the furniture warehouse
I said, "Well... you are a tall boy!"

He said, "Can I be of assistance?
Or offer a little advice?
Now if it's a sofa you're after
Well, this one's especially nice,
Upholstered in sultry black leather
And done round the edges in chrome
And I know it withstands shocking treatment
For I happen to have one at home."

Oh I know it was wrong but I liked him;
I knew he would lead me astray.
And yet as the sun caught his earring
I heard myself saying, "Okay."
When he asked me to go to the pictures
And ignoring his customers' glares
I said, "Is it Studio One then or Two?"
He said, "Studio Three. That's upstairs."

So I met him that Saturday evening
I went all dressed up in me prime.
He brought me a fragile white orchid
And a drink on a stick at half time.
He bought me a carton of popcorn
Our eyes met as I prised up the lid.
"Oh thank you," I said to him softly
And he laughed and said, "Stick with me... kid."

We went for a Chinese and there in the dark,
To the clang of the Chinese top ten,
"Your beauty," he said, "has gone to my head
With the sweet and sour pork." Oh and then
He said, "Darlin' it's wrong, but I'll ask you,
Oh make all my cravings complete,
Instead of just buying a sofa
Why don't you invest in a suite?"

The Slimming Poem

I'm a slimmer by trade, I'm frequently weighed,
I'm slim as a reed in the river.
I'm slender and lean, and hungry and mean.
Have some water, it's good for your liver.

Don't give me cheese rolls or profiteroles
Don't show me that jelly a-shakin',
Don't give me cream crackers you picnic and snackers
Or great big ice-creams with a flake in.

Don't give me swiss roll or toad-in-the-hole
Don't show me that Black Forest gateau.
You sit and go mouldy you old garibaldi
Your pastry all riddled with fat. Oh!

When I'm fat I feel weary and tubby and dreary
The stairs make me struggle and grunt dear,
And yet I'm so happy and punchy and snappy
When me hip bones are stuck out the front dear.

No, it's white fish for me, no milk in me tea
And if we don't like it we lump it.
No figs or sultanas, no mashed-up bananas
No pleasure and no buttered crumpet.

So don't get any bigger, me old pear-shaped figure
I can and I will become thinner.
So cheer up and take heart, pass the calorie chart,
Let's see what we're having for dinner!

Take Me Back
to Old Littlehampton

I didn't *want* to come on holiday
I know I shan't enjoy it
If I think of any way to hamper yours
Then I'll employ it.
I didn't like the journey
And I don't like our hotel
And I wished I'd stayed at home
That would have done me very well.

No! I am *not* going swimming
Not with my infected ear
Not with all those half-dressed women
Running up and down, no fear.
I'll just sit here in the bedroom
Oh and pull the curtains, do
For the sun inflames me headache
Oh it's all very well for you!

You go and have a lovely time
Don't think of me at all
No, I've got me English paper
You go out and have a ball
You go and have a rave up!
Go on! Go and have a fling!
But don't come for me at dinner time
I couldn't eat a thing.

Last night I ate that gastro-enteritis on a plate
I thought I'd make it to the Ladies,
But no, I was too late.
Go on! Enjoy your dinner!
Have the fish oil and the wine!
But buy some Alka Seltzer:
I shan't give you one of mine!

I could have been at home now
Sitting watching the TV
With me hair all washed and set
And with the cat sat on me knee.
I can't use me heated rollers
For the volts are up the creek
And the bath's all full of sand
I haven't had one for a week!

Still, it's all right, no it's lovely,
And we saved up for a year.
Dear Mother, having a lovely time
I wish that you were here.
How I let myself be talked
Into a fortnight I dunno,
Still you go out — enjoy it!
One week down. And one to go.

33

The Stanford Mafia

Oh I'm tired of pushing a pen
And writing poems round the place.
I think I'll have a change
And undergo a *volte-face*,
On considering the choice
Of an alternative career
What I'd most like to be
Is a protection racketeer.

I wouldn't want to do it
In the city or the town
For that is trespassing in gangland
And I s'pect I'd get mown down.
No, I'd stay out in the country
It's where I prefer to be.
I'm your friendly neighbourhood mugger
In your area — fly me.

We would not be extortionate
At all you understand,
But me and Angel Face Scarlatti'd
Sort of amble round the land
Saying, "We haven't come to murder you
Or worry you or con ya!
No, we're just passing through
We've come to put the finger on ya!"

I'd see that Mrs Lilly Sprocket —
Now I happen to know she knits
Oh the usual things, the bonnets
And the booties and the mitts —
Saying, "I don't want no trouble Lilly,
Trouble? Me? Bless your old soul!
But how much *is* it worth
To see your Knitmaster stay whole?"

There's a lovely market garden
Up the road at Rushy Weir,
We could go and case the joint
And say, "Nice place you got down here."
I could take along a breeze block
Which I casually could toss
Straight through the greenhouse roof
To help the message get across.

We could go and see the farmer
With his golden fields of grain,
"Wotto, me dear," I'd say,
"I see we haven't had much rain.
I run a little service,
Dunno what you think it's worth,
I go round dousing people's blowlamps
If they've come to scorch your earth."

A protection racketeer!
Me brim turned down about me eyes,
I'd drive a mighty Buick
And I'd say, "Okay you guys,"
I'd puff me old cheroot,
Turn up me collar past me ear.
This is Pam Ayres of the underworld!
…Nice place you got down here….

The Car Wash
Black and Blues

Oh Dad, Oh please don't send me down the Car Wash
Just like you send me every Friday night
For on seeing the mechanical contrivance
I find that I am overcome with fright.
I put my fifty pence into the slot Dad
And as the mechanism starts to go,
The last thing that I see before the darkness
Is the wash attendant saying, "Cheerio."

And it's black Dad, black as night inside the Car Wash,
And every time I realize too late
That the wireless aerial's not in the socket
And before my eyes it scribes a figure eight.
I know it's quick Dad, speedy and efficient,
Them brushes clean the car from head to feet
But they also get the windscreen wipers Daddy
And flick them half a mile across the street.

Them rubbers Dad, they're slapping at the window
I know they're supposed to make the paintwork gleam,
But I am thinking Dad in all the racket
Will anybody *hear* me when I scream?
It's proper claustrophobic in the Car Wash
Them brushes Dad are sinister and black
If the front one doesn't lift the lid and get you,
Another one is rolling up the back.

You haven't got a coward for a son Dad,
For all the times my back you've gaily slapped,
It's just that with the Car Wash coming at me
I sort of get the feeling that I'm trapped.
And all that drumming Dad, it isn't water
It's hot wax spraying all around the place,
One day I left the quarterlight ajar Dad
And hot wax spattered all across me face.

Oh Dad, don't let us patronize the Car Wash
Let's go back to our old-fashioned plan,
Washing it ourselves on Sunday morning
With a squirt of Fairy liquid in the can.
Don't send me down the Car Wash any more Dad,
Send my sister, send my cousin Alf,
Send someone insensitive and stupid
Or alternatively, drive it there yourself!

In 1978, the Health and Safety Executive launched a campaign aimed at reducing the number of injuries sustained by children playing on building sites. I was sent a horrific list of accidents, many of them fatal, which had befallen these children, and I was asked to contribute something in verse form to the campaign. This was my reason for writing "Building Sites Bite!".

Building Sites Bite!

This is a horror story
And it's worse because it's true.
Dan Sandheap and Fred the Hole
Have come to talk to you,
Claude the concrete mixer,
Mick the Brick and Cable Man
Have come here from a building site
To warn you if they can.

Claude the concrete mixer
Came up shuffling to the front
He said, "All day on building sites
It's back and forth I shunt.
The workmen prop me up
And rush away to eat their lunch,
So you play under me
So I can fall upon you... CRUNCH!"

Fred the Hole spoke up,
His voice as deep as any grave,
"Climb in me one rainy day
And down the walls will cave!
I'll trap you in the bottom
Where no one can hear you shout
Or see you in the mud and muck
Nor run to get you out."

Dan the Sandheap piped up with,
"They think they're at the sea
When they spy my lovely sand
They run and climb on me
And then I tumble down on them
All slippery and seething.
I cover them in sand and soon
I can't hear any breathing...."

For building sites are dangerous
Great lorries rush about
And just one lick from Mick the Brick
Is sure to knock you out.
Cable Man said, "I'm just one
Bare wire here alone
But touch me with your fingers
And I'll burn you, skin and bone."

On building sites these rotten creatures live
And many more
So please don't *play* on building sites
It's not what they are for.
They're full of dangers everywhere
Scattered all about
Too many children venture in
And never come back out.

The Wasp He Is a Nasty One

The wasp he is a nasty one
He scavenges and thrives,
Unlike the honest honey bee
He doesn't care for hives.
He builds his waxy nest
Then brings his mates from near and far
To sneak into your house
When you have left the door ajar.

Then sniffing round for jam he goes,
In every pot and packet,
Buzzing round the kitchen
In his black and yellow jacket.
If with a rolled-up paper
He should spot you creeping near
He will do a backward somersault
And sting you on the ear!

You never know with wasps,
You can't relax, not for a minute
Whatever you pick up — Look out!
A wasp might still be in it.
You never even know
If there's a wasp against your chest,
For wasps are very fond
Of getting folded in your vest.

And he *always* comes in summer.
In the winter-time he's gone
When you never go on picnics
And you've put a jersey on.
I mean, what other single comment
Causes panic and despair
Like someone saying, "Keep still!
There's a wasp caught in your hair!"

But in a speeding car
He finds his favourite abode
He likes poor Dad to swat like mad
And veer across the road.
He likes to watch Dad's face,
As all the kids begin to shout,
"Dad! I don't like wasps!
Oh where's he gone, Dad? Get him *out*!"

And I'd like to make a reference
To all the men who say,
"Don't antagonize it
And the wasp will go away,"
For I've done a little survey
To see if it will or won't,
And they sting you if you hit them
And they sting you if you don't.

As we step into the sunshine
Through the summers and the springs,
Carrying our cardigans
And nursing all our stings,
I often wonder, reaching for the blue bag
Just once more,
If all things have a purpose
What on earth can *wasps* be for?

41

The Railway Carriage Couple

Our home's a railway carriage
And it cannot be denied
That you might describe our dwelling
As a little bit on the side.
Yet it has the odd advantages
Where other housing fails,
And we're on the straight and narrow
So we can't go off the rails!

Our decor is original
It's simple but it's good
With little plaques screwed on the wall
That give the type of wood.
And up above the headrest
Of the seat marked number five
Is a photograph of Cheddar Gorge
In case we don't arrive.

Yes we're the railway carriage couple
With the long drive at the front,
Or it might be at the back
If we feel like a change, and shunt.
We're a little isolated
But if ever I get bored
And feel like communicating
I stand up and pull the cord.

I don't do much entertaining,
It's too cramped you see by far
For dining graciously
Because it's not a buffet car,
So we eat out in the corridor
My husband doesn't care
But I like to face the engine
Even though it isn't there.

Of course there is a certain problem
Which we have and always will
In that we cannot use the toilet
While the train is standing still.
So we built one just beside us
And we glazed it in with glass.
The first time my husband used it
He came back and said, "First class!"

We have a little garden
We don't buy much in the town,
You can see us any evening
Raking clinker up and down.
You might see us in our door
If you don't travel by too fast,
And we'll let down two holes in the leather strap
And wave as you go past.

Oh love, you got no poke left
I didn't want to say
It seems we are outmoded,
Much too slow, and in the way.
You know how much I love you
I'd repair you in a flash
But I haven't got the knowledge
And I haven't got the cash.

There is rust all round your headlamps
I could push through if I tried
My pot of paint can't cure it
'Cause it's from the other side.
All along your sides and middle
You are turning rusty brown
Though you took me ninety thousand miles
And never let me down.

Not the snapping of a fan belt
Nor the blowing of a tyre
Nor the rattling of a tappet
And nor did you misfire.
All your wheels stayed on the corners
And your wipers on the screen
Though I didn't do much for you
And I never kept you clean.

All your seats are unupholstered
And foam rubber specks the floor.
You were hit by something else once
And I cannot shut the door.
But it's not those things that grieve me
Or the money that I spent,
For you were my First-driven,
Ninety thousand miles we went.

I could buy a bright and new car
And go tearing round the town
A BGT! A Morgan!
(With the hood all battened down).
But as I leave you in the scrapyard,
Bangers piled up to the skies,
Why do your rusty headlamps
Look like sad, reproachful eyes?

Good-bye
Worn Out
Morris
1000

Ned Sails in the Sunset

Don't play me them nostalgic ballads Eunice,
You know it breaks my aching heart in two,
You know it makes me think of darlin' Neddy
And how such men are far between... and few.
I still can see him standing on the quayside,
In his uniform and all, he looked so grand
With gold braid gleaming all around his helmet
And a cornish pastie steaming in his hand.

"Good-bye my love!" he cried, his throat constricted,
"You are my comfort and my sustenance!"
He faltered and I thought emotion choked him
But he'd tried to eat the pastie all at once.
I held him and beseeched him, "Sail in safety!
Journey through the darkness to the light!
May Providence protect your tattered rigging
And hold your rudder steady in the night!"

He turned to board the craft, my heart was aching,
Crying, "Ned... shall I never see you more?"
But he brushed away the salt spray from his eyebrow
And resolutely shut the cabin door.
I watched his boat sail off into the sunset,
A thousand violins began to play,
And I thought I saw an old tomato sandwich
Tossing back and forth among the spray.

A mile off shore the fog came down to shroud him,
It hid the Channel ferry from his view,
It sliced his boat in half, the back and front end
And Ned was standing in betweeen the two.
They sent the air-sea rescue out to find him
But just a cornish pastie stayed afloat.
Don't play me them nostalgic ballads Eunice
For Ned and I are severed... like his boat.

A - Z

Driving in London's my pleasure
I prize it above any other,
One hand on the wheel
The fingers like steel
And the *A - Z* clenched
In the other.